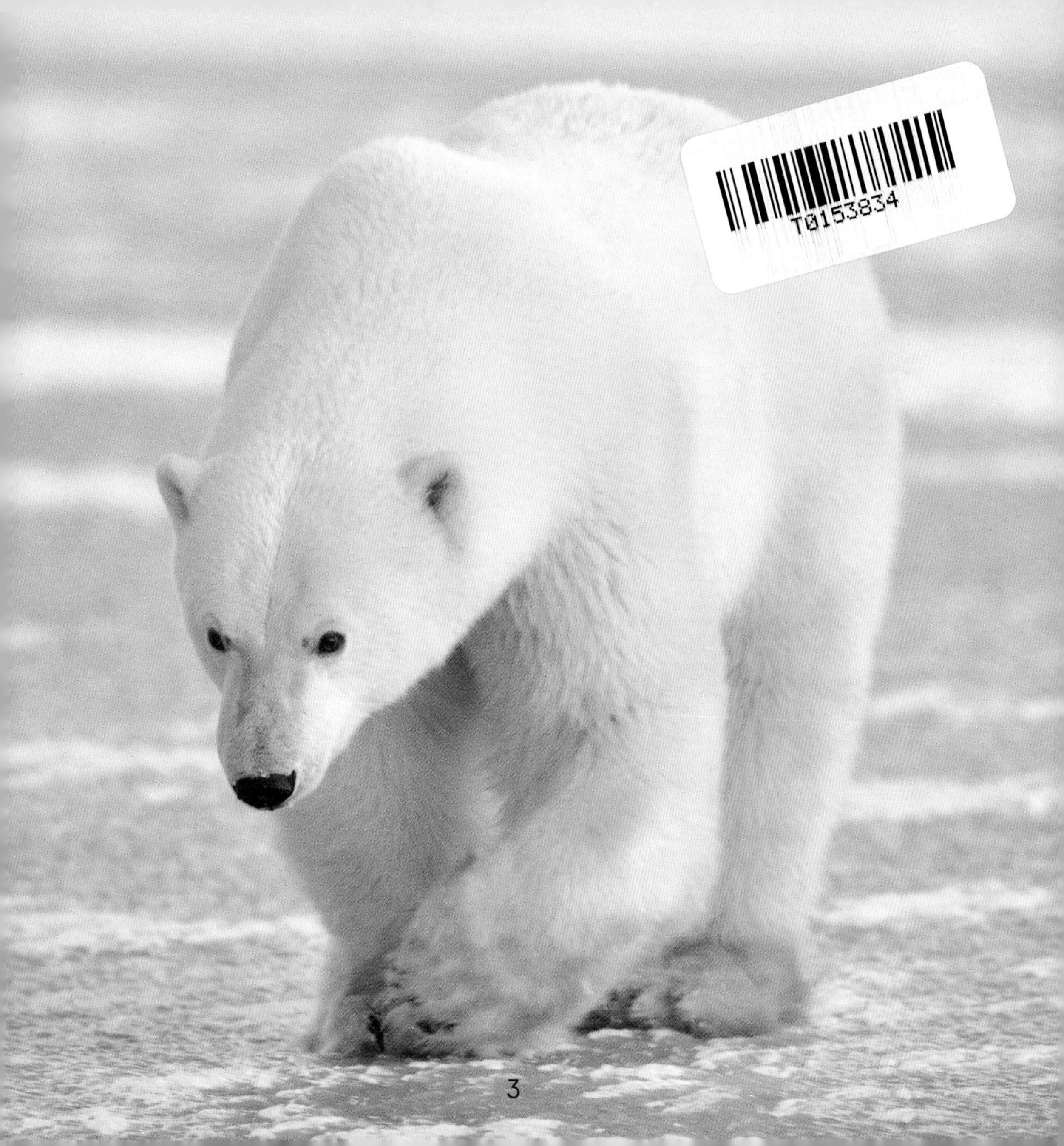

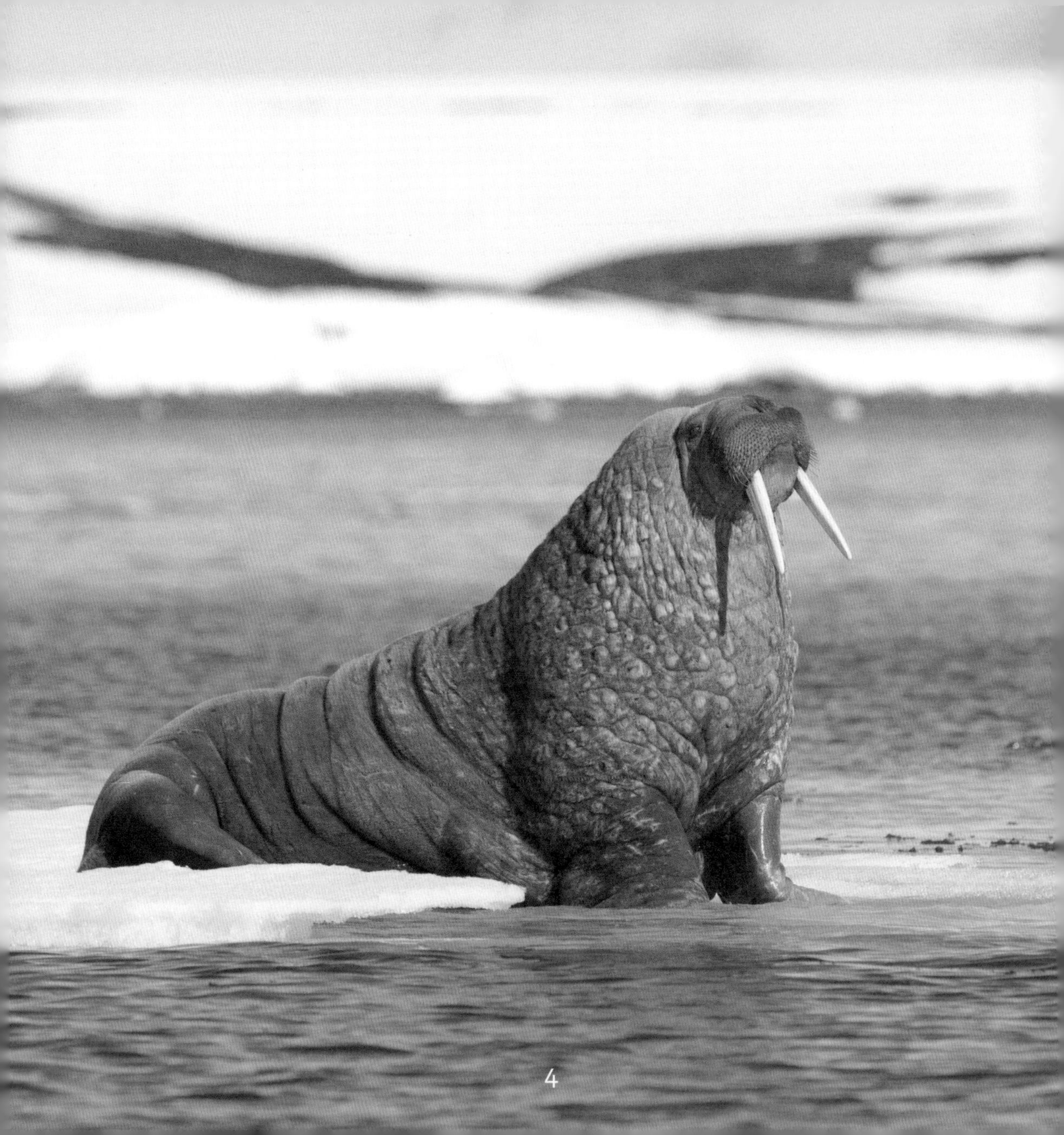

walrus

wolf

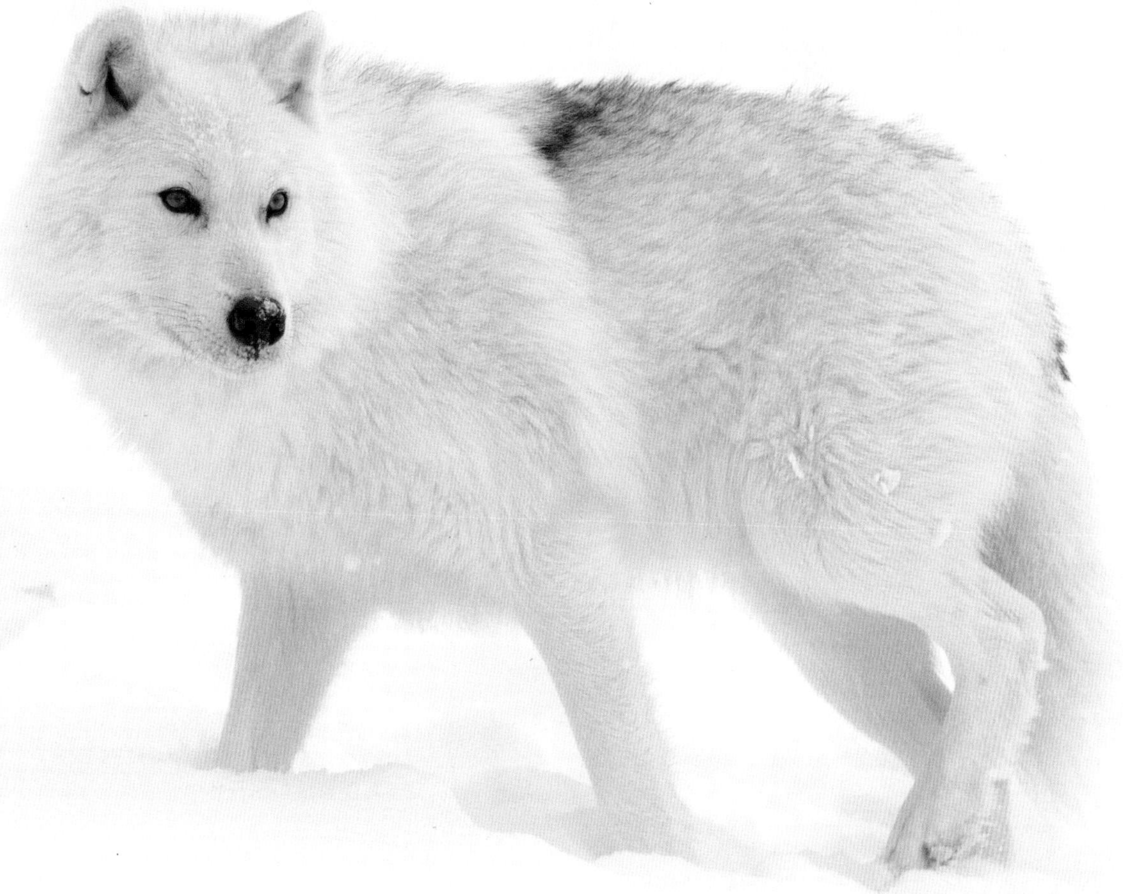

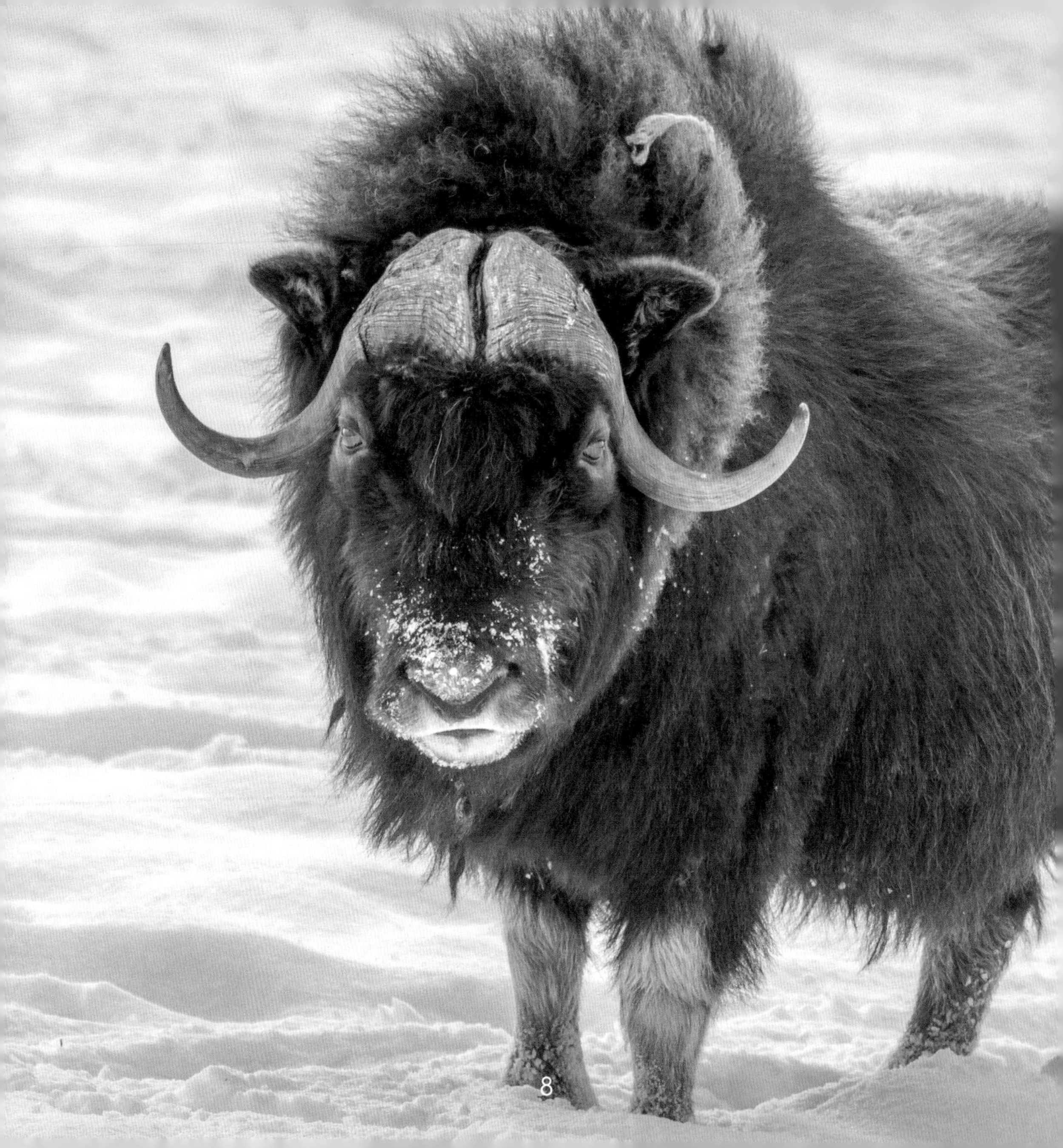

muskox

caribou

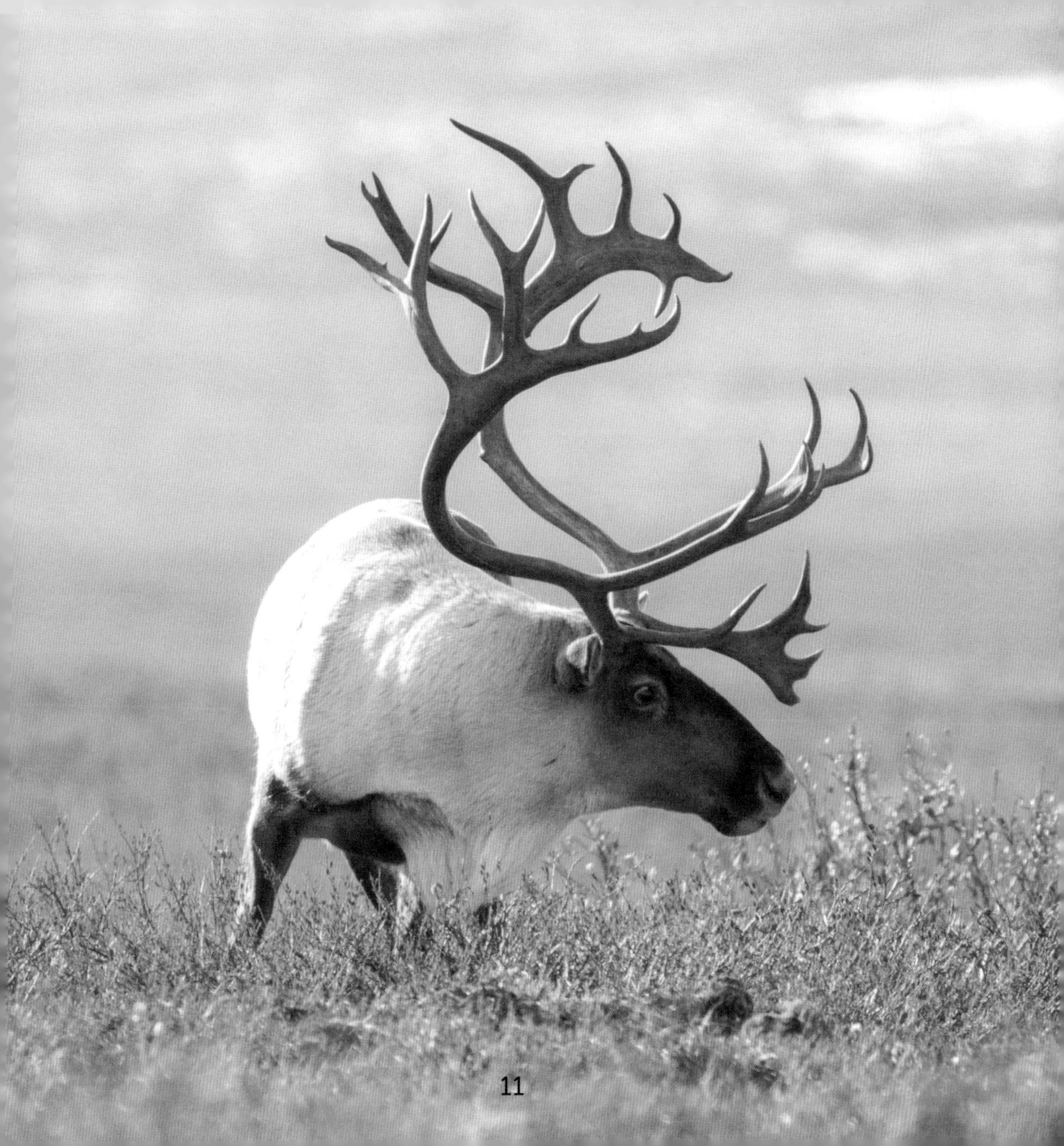

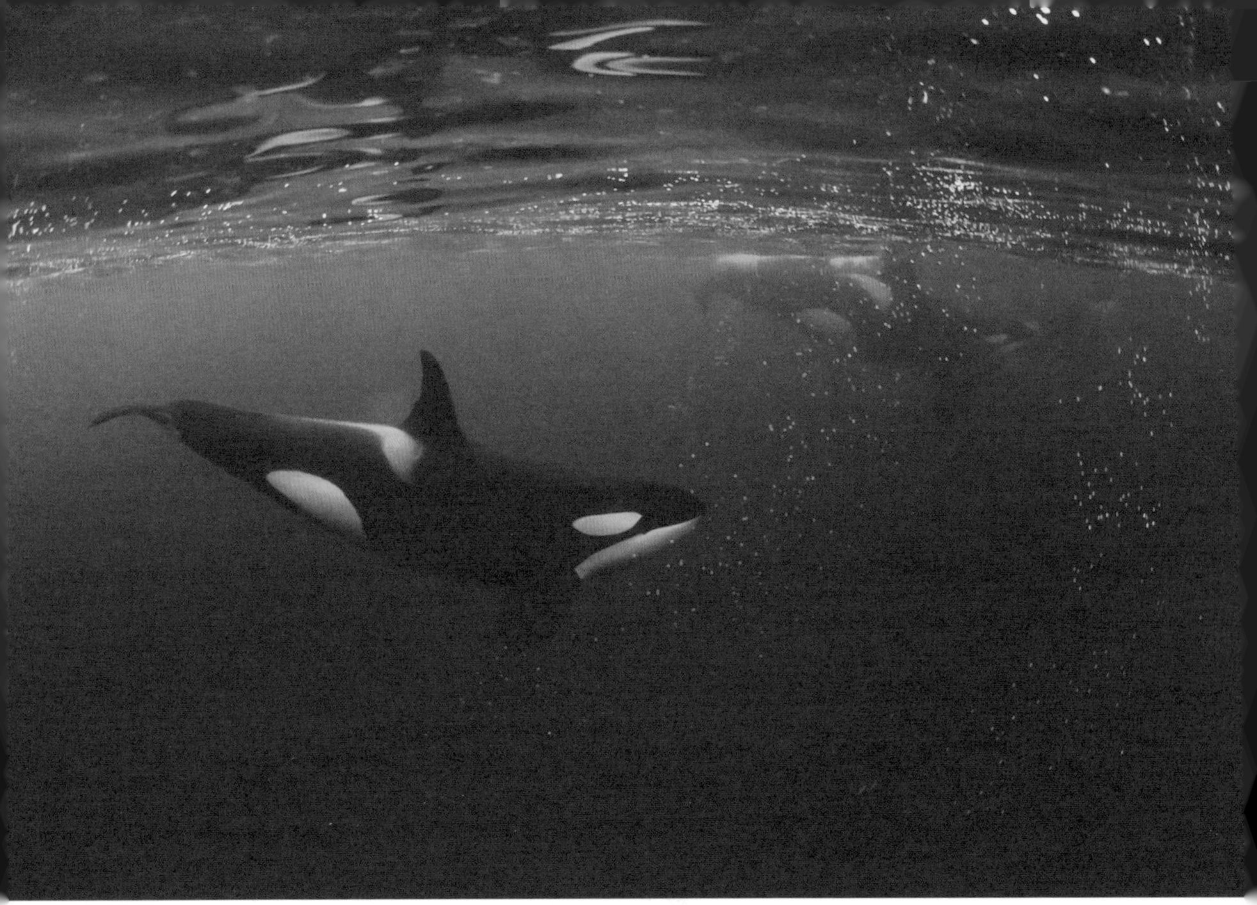

orca

Big Animals
in the Arctic

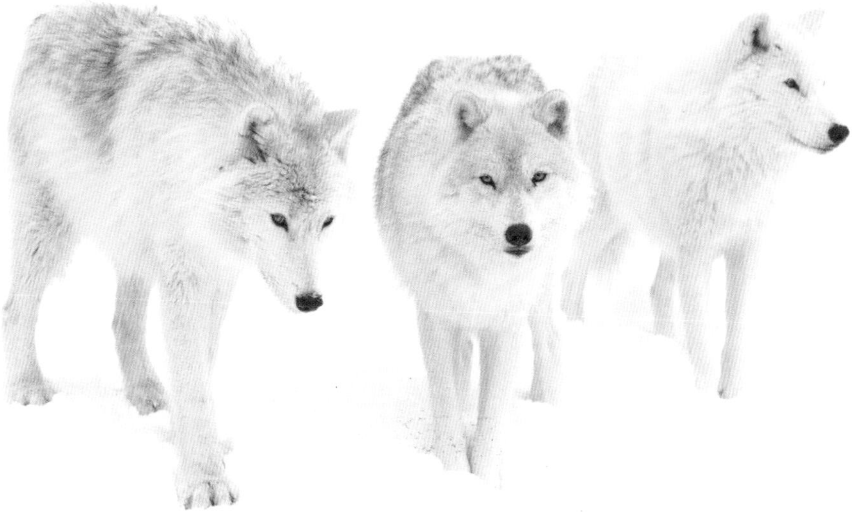

polar bear